CAPE

Inua Ellams

CAPE

OBERON BOOKS
LONDON
WWW.OBERONBOOKS.COM

First published in 2013 by Oberon Books Ltd
521 Caledonian Road, London N7 9RH
Tel: +44 (0) 20 7607 3637 / Fax: +44 (0) 20 7607 3629
e-mail: info@oberonbooks.com
www.oberonbooks.com

PB ISBN: 978-1-78319-066-9
E ISBN: 978-1-78319-565-7

Cover design by Inua Ellams

Synergy Theatre Project creates groundbreaking work which harnesses the energy, instincts and life experiences of those we work with – prisoners, ex-prisoners, young offenders and young people at risk of offending – gives them a voice and, in doing so, their dignity back. We inspire change by affecting feelings, attitudes and behaviour and provide practical opportunities which build a bridge from prison to social reintegration.

We are also concerned with the impact of our work on the public and use stories to humanise and provide new insights into the criminal justice system. Central to our approach is a commitment to artistic quality and empowerment of beneficiaries with the work taking place both in theatres and prisons and non-traditional venues, playing to diverse audiences and promoting mutual exchange between performers and audience to break down social barriers.

www.synergytheatreproject.co.uk

Company no: 4219146   Registered Charity: 1088692

The UK's theatre for young audiences

The Unicorn is the UK's leading professional theatre for young audiences, dedicated to inspiring and invigorating young people of all ages, perspectives and abilities, and empowering them to explore the world – on their own terms – through theatre.

Year-round, the Unicorn works with some of the world's most exciting theatre-makers to produce, present and tour a surprising, innovative and broad range of work that is honest, refreshing and international in outlook.

At the Unicorn, we believe in:
- bringing art to young people and young people to art
- pushing the boundaries of what theatre for young audiences can be
- opening our doors to everyone
- speaking to the audience of today, not just creating the audience of the future
- diversity. Because the world is diverse.

At the Unicorn, we strive to push the boundaries of imagination in everything that we do; welcoming families, schools, and young people for unforgettable theatrical experiences that will expand horizons, change perspectives, and challenge how we all see and understand each other.

Supported using public funding by
**ARTS COUNCIL
ENGLAND**

Commissioned and produced by Synergy Theatre Project with the Unicorn Theatre, *Cape* was first performed at the Unicorn on 19 November 2013 following a tour to schools, pupil referral units, prisons and a young offender institution.

Cast

BRUCE	Valentine Olukoga
TANYA	Letitia Wright
SMITHY	Laurence Mitchell
UHURU	Ricky Fearon
AMA	Diveen Henry

Director	Esther Baker
Designer	Katy McPhee
Sound Designer	Sarah Weltman
Video Designer	Chris Beston
Costume Designer	Sophia Simensky
Assistant Director	Neil Charles
Casting Director	Nadine Rennie CDG
Company Stage Manager	Rupert Carlile
Assistant Stage Managers	Michael Balogun, Daniel Harvey and Frank Prosper
Voice Coach	Kate Godfrey

Please note that the text of the play which appears in this volume may be changed during the rehearsal process and appear in a slightly altered form in performance.

Supported by

LOTTERY FUNDED

JOHN LYON'S
CHARITY

ACT 1

BRUCE: Tanya the more time you waste, the more time he's got to get away. Just tell me what I need /

TANYA: I'm setting the scene, the best writers do that.

BRUCE: Just get to the point. WHO DID IT?!

TANYA: But that's not the point!

BRUCE: God! You're so... COME ON TANYA!

TANYA: No Bruce, I'm not telling you like that.

BRUCE: And what's with the whole action and cut thing?

TANYA: Coz it's like a film...what happened. It's not clear like... and whatisname should direct it...who made Batman?

BRUCE: Christopher Nolan

TANYA: Yeah...multiple camera angles, story lines, stunts, body doubles and stuff

BRUCE: What? You gonna sell the story?

TANYA: Why not? It's a good one.

BRUCE: *(Laughs.)* Nutter.

TANYA: Isn't it?

BRUCE: You're mad Tanya.

TANYA: Admit it!

BRUCE: Just tell me who so I can…please Tanya?

TANYA: Naa Bruce, that won't help, you gotta listen, just trust me.

BRUCE: Tanya if you don't /

TANYA: You're not sure who it is, so you can't do anything. You're stuck here, might as well listen.

BRUCE: I…fine…whatever.

TANYA: Yesss… Okay, I'll start from the top.

A simple bus stop on a side street at night, old lottery tickets litter the ground like large confetti. On the red plastic bench, someone's written 'eff the police' with a thick black marker, there's a bin spilling parking tickets out across the street and the one florescent light is blinking. There's a mother /

BRUCE: OUR mother.

TANYA: Fine then, Mum, Uhuru Moses,

BRUCE: Yep.

TANYA: And a police man.

BRUCE: Constable Smith

TANYA: Yeah, but they don't know him yet.

BRUCE: They don't?

TANYA: Don't think so.

BRUCE: Okay…alright. Mum, PC Smith and Uhuru Moses. Carry on.

TANYA: Gotta do it properly…

Scene, characters, Aaaaaaannnnd Action!

// SMITHY is aggressive, shouting almost, UHURU speaks calmly, AMA is scared –

SMITHY: We who police this land, these streets, take our jobs very seriously!

UHURU: Ama, stand back from this lunatic.

SMITHY: We execute the law with utmost clarity.

UHURU: How many black men have died in police custody? Is that your clarity?

SMITHY: We cannot be held accountable for the actions of a few.

UHURU: Stop and Search policy? You treat entire communities as criminals because of the actions of a few.

AMA: Gentlemen, calm down.

SMITHY: That is a preventative measure.

AMA: Uhuru, step back from the policeman.

UHURU: You want to prevent crime? First, stop supporting a system that directly necessitates crime; politicians who are criminals, companies breaking tax laws /

SMITHY: That is a separate issue.

UHURU: Really? Let me link them for you.

// A figure dressed in black jumps from the shadows and attacks AMA. SMITHY, on hearing her scream pulls out a truncheon and smacks the figure till the figure falls and keeps swinging, frustration pouring out onto the figure.

SMITHY: Arghh stop! Stop it! Stop that! That's not what happened and you know it. Think we're heartless, stone cold bastards, wifed to violence, think we've no conscience? Love our batons? Breaking knuckles? Cracking heads? Blood on pavements, think we're like this? I believe in justice; it's a honourable thing, this badge means we uphold justice, protect what we love, that's our task, police the country, protect its bridges, alleys, tunnels, streets, even the bus stops. Some nights in the squad car, when everything is still, there's a quietude, a tranquility settles on the city. A sleeping urban forest, litter like fallen leaves, puddles are small rivers, street lights are trees, and we ensure the predators are in prison. That's the job. That's the collar. The light with the dark, the weight on our shoulders and when we're successful, people forget we exist, good policing is invisible, I'm fine with that, that's the system and it works…most of the time. When it doesn't, things are upturned and this is what happens. This is outside the system…and… permission to speak freely? Commander, this whole disciplinary hearing is a farce. My record is clean. I've been an outstanding copper since I joined the force and it is their word against mine. The individual Uhuru Moses was inciting violence and Bruce Okafor was his students, as was his mother. Bruce and I crossed paths a few times. I saw him on the night in question as I had many nights before. The first time we met, I sent him home. Perhaps I was a little...heavy handed, but nothing to warrant a complaint and no more than was necessary to get the job done. He was angry Commander, he roamed the streets taking the law into his own hands. His mother was mugged a month before and he'd started hunting the culprit but four weeks ago he became obsessive, dark, we met that Friday, third time that week.

BRUCE: Go solve a proper crime, don't get in my way.

SMITHY: If I see you again tonight, I'll bring you in for your own safety.

BRUCE: He's still out there prowling, animal in shadows, waiting for prey. If that was your Mum, what would you do? Chill at home? Watching CSI? Ain't doing that.

SMITHY: I understand your anger.

BRUCE: So let me protect mine and you protect yours.

SMITHY: That's our job.

BRUCE: What? To protect me?

SMITHY: Yes!

BRUCE: So why you on me then? Do I look like a criminal?

SMITHY: I have a son your age, I know how you feel... what you're going through

BRUCE: Get off me.

SMITHY: I'm sorry. You okay?

BRUCE: I need protection from you.

SMITHY: You have to go home now.

BRUCE: You all know who did it, if you don't find him, I will.

SMITHY: Go.

BRUCE: And after that I came home Tanya.

TANYA: It didn't hurt?

BRUCE: Naa…if it did, I was too angry to notice. I walked home, feeling lucky he didn't found the screwdriver in my pocket! Hahaha. I can't bring myself to take a knife. Came home thinking this whole area has changed. Time when played football all-day Sunday, ice lollies, kicking against the wall, corner of Beston Street /

TANYA: Yeah, that was nice.

BRUCE: The whole place was nice, the only thing lurking in the shadows was dying flowers, bleached grass and litter. All that's changed, no more strolling home at night from Ahmed's, eyes glazed from PlayStation and you, no more skipping casually from choir, taking ages

TANYA: Man!

BRUCE: It's not safe. Remember Mum the day after the mugging, when the pastor came round? Shaking in the living room?

AMA: Hello Pastor. Thanks for coming to visit me at home. I'm sorry, I don't think I'll come on Sunday… I won't have the strength. I appreciate your time. I talked with the victim support unit. They've been caring, really attentive, they've listened so much… I was surprised, given what you hear of the police these days. They are great, but I needed to talk to someone I know. I can't talk to the kids, can't have them worried, so thanks for coming. It was dark Pastor, it always is in stories like this. I had the shopping, I was walking to the car. He came from the shadows, a blur of fists and venom, spitting insults. Swear words. Threats. His voice wasn't raised. Quiet forceful, like small sharp knives, many of them. I actually heard him running before I saw him, thought it was a jogger, that I'd breathe in his sweat as he flashed by but he grabbed me, slammed my head against the wall, twice. Threw me to the ground, put one foot on my back so I couldn't turn. Crushing me, pushing air from my lungs. Face down on the ground. I remember…chewing gums Pastor, flattened into the pavement, black with mud and soot. Hundreds of them. So many…mouths to feed, so many people walk this way, could have happened to any of them, but it happened to me. He bent over, mouth inches from my ears, making quiet demands after the insults. I said "You don't have to do this, I'll give you what you want, let an old woman stand up" but he punched the side of my face, twice. He emptied my bag by my head. Took my purse, cash, phone, bank cards. I gave my PIN number…he had my driving license, said he'd come visit if I lied. Told me not to get up, not to dare and he vanished. I stayed like that for thirty minutes. Shivering on the concrete. Didn't know when it started raining, but I was drenched when I stood. I tried singing Amazing Grace but couldn't recall the words. I staggered around, looking for help, swaying in the night, falling, standing again, trying to sing myself better. Someone found a policeman and his strong arms held me up. Can't remember his name but I'll recognise him if we meet. I'll thank him. A good man, spoke calmly, held me 'til a female police officer came. I haven't slept Pastor. I try, but jolt back, wake up, and see the mugger at the foot of my bed, threatening to come in, to find me again. Victim support say that I will feel this way, that it is natural, normal. But it shouldn't be Pastor. Why couldn't I remember the words? Where was grace? Where was God? My hands are shaking... Pastor... I can't stop shaking.

TANYA: You were eaves dropping, crying by the door.

BRUCE: No I wasn't.

TANYA: Yes you were. Don't be ashamed, I was scared too. Remember she tried to go outside the next day and ran back in, leaning against the wall, proper shook?

BRUCE: Yeah.

TANYA: She is better now.

BRUCE: Still hasn't talked to us about it.

TANYA: Maybe she doesn't need to, she's been going out.

BRUCE: She's putting on a brave face Tanya but there's been two more muggings since, violent ones, she must be a little scared...and I'm not playing anymore. No more pretend.

TANYA: No?

BRUCE: Naa, The mugger's out there and I'm not having him walk free.

TANYA: When do we start?

BRUCE: You can't come Tan. Not anymore.

TANYA: We planned for ages!

BRUCE: What? BlackMan and Ribbon? Wiping crime off the streets? You serious?

TANYA: I don't wear ribbons. It was your idea in the first place.

BRUCE: We were playing.

TANYA: I know but...they always have partners.

BRUCE: But this is real, and I ain't him. Can't watch you at the same time. Sorry.

TANYA: No cape then?

BRUCE: *(Laughs.)* Just my hoodie.

TANYA: Tool belt?

BRUCE: Just the torch light, screwdriver. The others will take ages to make.

TANYA: What about the taser? We finished that one.

BRUCE: Give it to Mum.

TANYA: She'll ask where we got it from.

BRUCE: Don't tell her we made it off a YouTube video! She'll never let you on the net! Just...tell her I got it off a friend, for her safety.

TANYA: She won't take it. She doesn't believe in violence.

BRUCE: It's not for violence. It's self-defence.

TANYA: Yeah...but you know Mum...tried talking to her about the self-defence class as well, told her martial arts is about discipline, showed her clips online, Bruce Lee talking about focusing the mind, spirituality and stuff but she said /

AMA: Naa... It's not for me. All that high-kicks and Hia! Hia! Hia! Eh eh... No. Thank you, but God will take care of me. Don't roll your eyes Tanya. When we had no money, God provided...church paid our rent.

TANYA: Okay Mum...just...please take the leaflet and read it? This one is just round the corner, the teacher was born round here? You might meet some other folks? Get a boyfriend?

AMA: Tanya!

TANYA: Just saying Mum! Just saying.

AMA: I don't need a man for anything.

TANYA: Protection?

AMA: God and my wrapper is all I need in this world.

TANYA: *(Laughs.)* Your wrapper?

AMA: It keeps me warm and it's beautiful. I used to wrap you and Bruce in something like this when you were babies. You should start wearing some you know? How about a scarf? I can cut a strip off?

TANYA: Naa mum, I'll get teased at school. But it'll make a nice fancy dress African superhero costume.

AMA: My clothes are not costumes.

TANYA: Didn't mean it like that.

AMA: Anyway, come down soon. Dinner is almost ready. Where's your brother?

TANYA: Er…he's gone out?

AMA: Where?

TANYA: PlayStation at Ahmed's.

AMA: PlayStation… I know when you are lying. Is he looking again?

TANYA: I…he's just trying to help.

AMA: Call that foolish boy, tell him to be here in ten minutes or else! A ah! That's the job of the police, he is not a trained detective, running around like a lunatic, he need to stay home and /

//AMA walks off mumbling to herself.

BRUCE: CUT CUT CUT! That was ages ago, thanks for defending me to Mum, lying for me…but you've gone off point Tanya. Smithy did it. Is that what you are saying?

ACT 2

BRUCE: Tanya?… Did Smithy do it?

TANYA: Sort of.

BRUCE: That's all I needed to know. Say Hi to Mum for me yeah?

TANYA: Wait! B, B! Bruce come back!

BRUCE: What?

TANYA: You can't go after him.

BRUCE: Far as I'm concerned, there's still a violent person out there and /

TANYA: He's Police Bruce!

BRUCE: Don't care.

TANYA: You can't just

BRUCE: Why not?

TANYA: He's Police!

BRUCE: Laters Tanya.

TANYA: Bruce wait! Mum was there too.

BRUCE: She had nothing to do with it.

TANYA: Have you talked to her?

BRUCE: She. Had. Nothing. To. Do. With. It.

TANYA: Wait! Mr Moses was there too and…lemme start from the top?

BRUCE: What? Again?

TANYA: Yeah.

BRUCE: Why?

TANYA: Just…trust me.

BRUCE: Don't have time.

TANYA: I'll be quick then?

It's important.

BRUCE: Okay.

TANYA: Cool…alright. PC Smith, Mum, Mr Moses. Scene, Characters…ac…you can say action if you want…

BRUCE: Tanya!

TANYA: C'mon B…

BRUCE: Fine. Action.

TANYA: A simple bus stop on a side street at night, old posters litter the ground like large confetti. On the red plastic bench, someone's written 'fight the power' with a thick black marker, there's a bin spilling leaflets out across the street and the one florescent light is blinking.

// UHURU is excited, animated as he talks. AMA is bored, unimpressed. SMITHY is calm.

UHURU: Money talks. If they don't have to pay law enforcement here, we save them money and given the austerity measures, that will count towards /

AMA: And what about the officers who will lose their jobs?

SMITHY: Yeah what about them?

UHURU: Who are you?

SMITHY: A concerned citizen.

UHURU: This is a private conversation, it doesn't concern you.

SMITHY: You're having it in a public space and /

AMA: Have we met before?

SMITHY: No. I don't think so. Now, Mr Moses, your proposal is preposterous. We will not accept any such /

AMA: No, we've met before. Before today. But you were at the meeting weren't you?

UHURU: Who do you mean by 'We'?

SMITHY: We who police this land, these streets, take our jobs very seriously.

UHURU: Ama, stand back from this lunatic.

SMITHY: We execute the law with utmost clarity.

UHURU: How many black men have died in police custody? Is that your clarity?

SMITHY: We cannot be held accountable for the actions of a few.

UHURU: Stop and Search policy? You treat entire communities as criminals because of the actions of a few.

AMA: Gentlemen, calm down.

SMITHY: That is a preventative measure.

AMA: Uhuru, step back from the policeman.

UHURU: You want to prevent crime? First, stop supporting a system that directly necessitates crime; politicians who are criminals, companies breaking tax laws /

SMITHY: That is a separate issue.

UHURU: Really? Let me link them for you.

// A figure dressed in black jumps from the shadows, attacks AMA. UHURU, on hearing her scream swiftly delivers punches and kicks to the figure, keeps on after the figure falls.

UHURU: Stop! That categorically didn't happen. Impossible. It would mean I lost control your Honour, allowed anger to own my bones, to rule movements but I teach control, I focus on focus so that never happened, I never attacked, I've never attacked. I learnt self defence. Never the hit-man. Never the drug dealer. Never the pimp. Never the cat burglar. Never loitered on streets. Never knew my father. But that never mattered, Mother was stronger than most men I knew, taught me never ever to steal, so the crocodile skins boots, I bought. Never diamonds, but Kugar rings, gold bracelets, duchet chains. I never wanted to start boxing, but the skin heads never stopped coming. Never loved England, England never loved me. Packed a bag and worked in Egypt. Never loved retail, a black man with fists? Worked in security for families, oil-rich kings, the ancients of Africa. They taught me our history. I taught their kids boxing, they paid for me to learn about Tai Chi, Taekwondo and Wing Chun. I never forget the lessons I learnt, how to watch your opponent, to spot them first, to stand guarded, to seek inner strength. Never forgot the friends I left and after ten years, I came to share the knowledge I'd gathered, the things I'd learnt. I came home. Never loved the gym so called mine a dojo, a place for my community and they came in droves. Still hanging punch bags, thirsty towels… floor mats, but never frenzy, never the heat. Still the commitment, the clenched fist focus, but never the anger, never the pain. Still the exertion, the sound of straining muscle, but never the swagger, never such pride. I never said no, all I asked was focus, taught a combination of Wing Chun and boxing. As I trained the young ones, they spoke their problems, the police officers, stop and search powers, deaths in custody, constant surveillance, threats to harmony, the new skinheads. I wanted to teach the history of our people, we came from royalty, a race of scholars, this country crushed our kingdoms, stole wealth and treats us like animals, treats us like filth. I never wanted politics your Honour, I had one goal: strengthen my community, protect my students, that was it. I welcomed them all, gangs that were enemies: train with your enemy, enemy becomes your friend, a stronger community, a tribe united, a people made whole. I taught inner strength, discipline and focus, lectured on action and consequence. If you are late, 50 press ups. No kit, 50 press ups. Thirsty? 50 press ups and they never complained. We start at 4 with

// As he talks, the class appears and run through the motions.

a warm up, skipping drills, the skill of the day, always end on breathing, light sparring or fast pad work.

UHURU: Ready Bruce?

BRUCE: Yes Mr Moses.

// They do a few combinations, getting faster, more intense, couple of times, UHURU hits BRUCE head a few ties as BRUCE is slow. After, the class bows.

UHURU: Okay. Hit the showers, see you next week. Bruce can I talk to you for a minute? What's wrong? Your intentions were right but focus wasn't there, you're all over the place.

BRUCE: Nothing sir.

UHURU: They still haven't found him?

BRUCE: No.

UHURU: Now Bruce /

BRUCE: I know what you're gonna say, but I can't stay in. There was another one last night? Two broken ribs. That's five now. Imagine if that was my sister /

UHURU: Be patient /

BRUCE: Tired of that. Police ain't doing nothing, I'm gonna find him. He never attacks during rush hour.

Waits till around nine thirty, ten. They've all happened like ten minutes from the station. If I get there around 9 and follow the most vulnerable looking person, I'm bound to catch him eventually.

UHURU: Bruce, let us help. You don't have to do this on your own. Since it started I've been thinking and... I'm holding a discussion in a few weeks for the locals, civilians, adults only, but I'll make an exception for you. We could use your help /

BRUCE: A few weeks?!

UHURU: These things take time.

BRUCE: I'll try and come but, doesn't mean I'll stop.

UHURU: I can't make you stop so...just be safe, be clear of your objective.

BRUCE: See you next week.

BRUCE: Tanya! Tanya! Anything to eat?

TANYA: Check the fridge!

BRUCE: Can't find anything!

TANYA: There's chips.

BRUCE: It's cold!

TANYA: It was in the fridge!

BRUCE: Cold chips for dinner? Erghu.

Where's Mum?

Mum? Mum!

TANYA: She left, like five minutes ago.

BRUCE: Out on a Wednesday night?

TANYA: Yeah…you don't know?

BRUCE: What?

TANYA: She started that martial arts class. The leaflet you gave me?

BRUCE: The adult class is straight after mine! Why'd she change her mind?

TANYA: She wouldn't take the taser and after the fifth mugging, guess she started thinking. Imagine. Mum doing karate chops! *(Laughs.)*

BRUCE: Man…can't wait to see her moves.

TANYA: It's the same guy right? The one that trains you?

BRUCE: Uhuru Moses.

TANYA: She's with him now. What's he like? Mum might get a boyfriend?

BRUCE: Na…too strict. Not Mum's type. He's smiled like once since I met him. Always focused, disciplined, like the black robcop of martial arts…afrocop.

TANYA: *(Laughs.)*

BRUCE: Seriously, like naa…in fact, Mum might drop out cause of how hard he is.

UHURU: *(Laughing.)* Mrs Okafor, you will kill me with these questions!

AMA: *(Laughing.)* They are obvious ones.

UHURU: Okay, okay. No, you won't be able to karate-chop someone into pieces.

AMA: That is unfortunate.

UHURU: You will not be able to jump over moving vehicles.

AMA: Not even that?

UHURU: No Mrs Okafor.

AMA: Miss Okafor.

UHURU: Miss Okafor.

AMA: So what will you teach me?

UHURU: We focus above all on discipline, focus and inner strength.

AMA: That won't help me in a fight. I want to bring him down like Mike Tyson.

UHURU: I don't teach boxing for the older groups.

AMA: I'm not old.

UHURU: I can see that, I mean…after a certain age, our bones require greater care and attention, our bones become for the finer things in life Miss Okafor.

AMA: Really Mr Moses. Call me Ama.

UHURU: Ama. A beautiful name.

AMA: You should hear my phone number.

UHURU: …

AMA: So, what exactly will you teach me?

UHURU: A combination of Tai Chi and Taekwondo.

AMA: You are sure I'll be able to defend myself?

UHURU: If after the fourth week, you cannot throw me to the ground, I will give you a full refund.

AMA: Brilliant! When do we start?

UHURU: Next week if you can make the class, but I do have a question Ama. Why do you want to learn? What's your motivation?

   – beat –

AMA: Good evening Pastor, thanks for seeing me at such short notice. I'm feeling better. The bruises have faded as you can see. The police support unit were brilliant. They check on me less often now and I no longer feel the need to talk about it. I still have relapses… sleepless nights, I wake up shivering, hear his voice knifing through me. I just feel angry. The unit say it's normal to feel this way. To feel embarrassed about my helplessness, that I did nothing, just lay, whimpering and took it. That's why I'm here Pastor. There've been more muggings. Our neighbours are twitchy, children nervous. Bruce is taking matters into his own hands… He is prowling around, fighting such darkness, it's my duty to show him light. It's affecting his schooling. I need to reassure him, to make Tanya feel safe…to feel secure, to overcome what happened. It's not about revenge… God will seek that, but 'Heaven helps those who help themselves' Remember Pastor? The sermon you preached? Well, this is how I want to help myself. Money, I can make, a phone came the next day… poverty, hunger, I understand the mugger's motives. But violence? To be attacked so mercilessly… I want to learn to stop that. To defend myself. To take lessons. What do you think Pastor? Do I have your blessing?

– *beat* –

UHURU: Ama? You okay?

AMA: Yes.

UHURU: My question, why do you want to learn?

AMA: Inner strength… It's good exercise…but truthfully Uhuru, above all I want to disarm men as strong and handsome as yourself.

UHURU: *(Laughs.)* Well…consider me disarmed Mrs Okafor.

AMA: Ama, please.

UHURU: My apologies, Ama.

BRUCE: Naa, doubt they'd get along. But he's a decent teacher.

TANYA: Just imagine Mum running out, dishing out karate-chops like cold chips. Drop-kicking everybody!

BRUCE: *(Laughs.)*

TANYA: Running around, some Nigerian-Superhero. "You there, drop that purse before I show you the dark side of my fist"

// TANYA runs around with AMA's wrapper tucked in her neckline, fighting invisible foes.

BRUCE: *(Laughs.)* Tanya you're killing me. But seriously, do you think she can?

TANYA: Huh?

BRUCE: Actually defend herself.

TANYA: Course.

BRUCE: Cause, you can learn techniques, stances, punches, combinations, all that…but when it's time, can you deliver? Mr Moses says fear is the worst human emotion, it immobilises us. We just stand and take it. Fear. If Mum is out and the mugger comes, will she fight?

TANYA: I dunno know.

BRUCE: Gotta make sure somehow.

TANYA: Maybe you and her should like do a session here? After she's done some classes?

BRUCE: But it's me though. She's not scared of me.

TANYA: Wear a mask or something.

BRUCE: She'll see me putting it on…like. No…that won't work.

TANYA: I know, MUG HER!

BRUCE: What?

TANYA: Just pretend…jump out the bushes on her way from work, see if she fights back.

BRUCE: You're crazy.

TANYA: Na… Bruce listen. Just shout and if she waves her fist, then you know she's cool.

BRUCE: Nuts Tanya. No.

TANYA: It'll work.

BRUCE: Listen I gotta go patrol.

TANYA: Think about it, it's the perfect way!

BRUCE: I'm going now Tanya. You're crazy.

TANYA: Wait! Wait! What about dinner?

BRUCE: Don't like cold chips.

TANYA: Wait! Wait!

BRUCE: What?

TANYA: You forgot your cape.

  // *TANYA throws over his hoodie.*

BRUCE: Thanks.

BRUCE: And I'm out stalking the urban forest, skimming alleys, flight footed and winged over banisters, climbing railings, quiet, quick when I need to be. Slow when I feel, casual, blending, watching, waiting, feeling these streets breathing with me.

SMITHY: And I'm out stalking the urban forest, driving down alleys, cruising main street, a symbol of order, justice, peace, slow when I drive, fast when I need, professional, visible, watching, waiting, feeling the streets breathing with me.

BRUCE: I'd do anything to keep this peace, this silent sleeping sweeping scene, lamp lights flickering, a couple kissing, the odd car passing like a lost ship, this hour of night you look for strange winds, a weird shaped shadow, anything that glints, I head north, turn down Duggan Way.

SMITHY: I'd do anything to keep this peace, this silent sleeping sweeping scene, traffic lights green, a couple kissing, the odd cyclist passing like a lost bird at sea, this hour of night, you look for strange winds, a weird shaped shadow, anything that glints. I head south, turn down Lawrence Street.

BRUCE: Up past the factory. Left down Benton. Right past Corn Way. Up through the square.

SMITHY: Up past the cemetery. Left down Charles. Right past Sun Way. Up through the square.

BRUCE: And I see him, a slouching shadow of a figure, leaning in shadows, waiting in the dark.

SMITHY: And I see him, a slouching shadow of a figure, leaning in shadows, waiting in the dark.

BRUCE: I rest up, catch my breath around the corner, waiting till he moves, taking my time.

SMITHY: I park up, in the alley round the corner, waiting till he moves, taking my time.

BRUCE: And I'm on him, running, he's fast, but I'm faster, clear headed, focused, bastard mugged my mum.

SMITHY: And I'm on him, running, he's fast, but I'm faster, clear headed, focused, hand around my baton.

// SMITHY grabs BRUCE, they struggle till SMITHY successfully pins him down, strikes him a couple of times till he is still, but moaning. SMITHY pulls down BRUCE's mask.

SMITHY: You?! Not again. I told you to stay off the streets. I told him to stay off the streets.

// As SMITHY addresses the Commander, BRUCE limps home. TANYA tends to his wounds.

SMITHY: No Commander, I didn't set out to find him, that's a false statement. His bruises were from the pavements, I tackled him hard. It was dark, I restrained the suspect; that's all he was. I un-cuffed him, gave another warning, told him to get lost. I didn't file a report. I thought it was pointless. He's not a bad kid and he didn't press charges... What old case? Yes I remember, Yes I brought him in. Domestic abuse. He was wounded in custody? Not on my watch. Three broken ribs? Okay, but not from me. I had nothing to do with that. Gotta be joking. What are you insinuating? Come on, spell it out. Commander what are you saying? What's this all about?

BRUCE: CUT.

– beat –

TANYA: You were really hurt that night Bruce. You got a
   fever. And Mum knew.

BRUCE: She did?

TANYA: Yeah. She entered the room. You were asleep…
   saw me wiping sweat from your face. Saw plasters,
   tissues. Blood. Heard her crying in her room, asking
   God what to do.

BRUCE: I…didn't know.

   - beat -

But again, that was in the past Tanya. The Bus Stop.
You saying it wasn't PC Smithy? Cause if it is… I get
that, but Mr Moses…if it's him… I can't…like…he's
my teacher.

ACT 3

BRUCE: You saying it was Mr Moses?

TANYA: No!

BRUCE: What then?! You're confusing me Tanya!

TANYA: I'm saying both of them were there! Both. Papers say the wounds were 'consistent'…means they matched right?

BRUCE: You read the papers?

TANYA: They were everywhere… I had to research! Watch when I sell the story.

BRUCE: It's not funny Tanya. I wish I could remember. My head still hurts…still bruised all over.

TANYA: You'll get better.

BRUCE: Oh Tanya… I… I'll get them back. That's what I'll… So Mr Moses as well? Fine.

TANYA: Bruce! Come back! What you gonna do when you see him?

BRUCE: Don't know but that's two attackers and it's not safe.

TANYA: Three.

BRUCE: What?

TANYA: Three people were there. Mum.

BRUCE: She had nothing to do with it.

TANYA: Bruce.

BRUCE: Not listening.

TANYA: Bruce.

BRUCE: Tanya.

TANYA: Bruce…

>   She's been different since it happened. Even worse than before.

BRUCE: I… I know but /

TANYA: Just listen okay?

BRUCE: Tanya there's no point /

TANYA: Gonna start from the top.

>   Same thing yeah?

BRUCE: No Tanya /

TANYA: Action.

>   *A simple bus stop on a side street at night, supermarket vouchers litter the ground like large confetti. On the red plastic bench, someone's written 'Moms rule ' with a thick black marker, there's a bin spilling tissues out across the street and the one florescent light is blinking.*

// AMA is flirting with UHURU, who speaks arrogantly. SMITHY is nervous.

AMA: The government will not accept any such proposal.

SMITHY: Hmm

UHURU: Money talks. If they don't have to pay law enforcement here, we save them money and given the austerity measures, that will count towards

AMA: And what about the officers who will lose their jobs?

SMITHY: Yeah what about them?

UHURU: Who are you?

SMITHY: A concerned citizen.

UHURU: This is a private conversation, it doesn't concern you.

SMITHY: You're having it in a public space and /

AMA: Have we met before?

SMITHY: No. I don't think so. Now, Mr Moses, your proposal is preposterous. We will not accept any such /

AMA: No, we've met before. Before today. But you were at the meeting weren't you?

UHURU: Who do you mean by 'We'?

SMITHY: We who police this land, these streets, take our jobs very seriously.

UHURU: Ama, stand back from this lunatic.

SMITHY: We execute the law with utmost clarity.

UHURU: How many black men have died in police custody? Is that your clarity?

SMITHY: We cannot be held accountable for the actions of a few.

UHURU: Stop and Search policy? You treat entire communities as criminals because of the actions of a few.

AMA: Gentlemen, calm down.

SMITHY: That is a preventative measure.

AMA: Uhuru, step back from the policeman.

UHURU: You want to prevent crime? First, stop supporting a system that directly necessitates crime; Politicians who are criminals, companies breaking tax laws /

SMITHY: That is a separate issue.

UHURU: Really? Let me link them for you.

// A figure dressed in black jumps from the shadows, attacks AMA. AMA falls on the floor as the men watch stunned. The figure towers over her, she reaches into her bag, pulls out the taser and attacks the figure repeatedly.

AMA: Stop! Stop! The rumours aren't true Pastor. I didn't seek vengeance, I'd never risk rippling the calm waters of our lives. How could I have known? You have to believe me. I'd never sink so low. To do to anyone what was done to me? Pastor, I'm not a danger, to anyone, especially my kids. I'm who God chose to keep them safe, their guardian, that's all I've ever done. After the eighth mugging Bruce became...and Tanya... Tanya adores her brother Pastor... I took it to appease them. I should have stuck to my principles, refused it blankly. I never thought I'd use it. But, against that wall, frightened, helpless...all over again...instincts took over. I lost control...my hand seemed to move by itself, reached into my bag...it was in my hand, a line of blue fire crackled and...but I couldn't have... It happened so fast. Was it my fault Pastor?... Was it me?... Okay... I'm fine...the last time I saw him? It was in the kitchen, the day it happened. I was ready for class, he was talking with Tanya. I entered the kitchen and they stopped.

TANYA: Hey Mum.

AMA: Hi Tanya.

Bruce?

It's like you don't live here any more.

Are you avoiding me?

Bruce I'm talking to you.

BRUCE: Mum, I know what you're gonna say.

AMA: You have to stop. I'm not blind you know. You are becoming so dark, a clenched fist of a human being. This is eating you...there will be nothing left.

BRUCE: Will you take the taser?

AMA: No

BRUCE: Then I can't stop. He's still out there.

AMA: It's not your job.

BRUCE: Cops are rubbish Mum. I'm trying to do something good yeah? I don't care what you, Mr Moses, Smithy or anyone says! Ain't waiting till he mugs Tanya!

AMA: Who is Smithy?

TANYA: Bruce, I'll be okay.

BRUCE: You don't know that Tan. He's getting us one by one...gotten away eight times now and we're just hiding indoors. If another person gets hurt, it's our fault. We're doing nothing!

AMA: I'm taking Uhuru's class.

BRUCE: And you'll fight back?

AMA: I pray I won't have to.

BRUCE: Hear that Tan? Hear that? This ain't about prayer. You have to be ready at all times yeah? Vigilant Mum. Be Vigilant. Take the taser. Take it.

AMA: No. No... Listen, when you step out that door, the whole world is waiting and it crashes and burns for someone everyday. Planes crash you know? Planes crash. Things drop out of the sky, any thing can go wrong any time. We are always on the verge of chaos and Bruce, running around at night is chaos too... We have to believe in something bigger than us and

God is order to my chaos. God watches, is vigilant for us all. He helps those who help themselves, so I am vigilant too…but that is one thing. Carrying weapons is another.

TANYA: But… Mum, God didn't help when the mugger was on you. If you had a taser…

AMA: Not you too… Tanya I thought /

TANYA: I'm just saying.

AMA: God works in mysterious ways.

BRUCE: Tell that to the mugger. Tell him God will go mysterious on him, maybe he'll stop.

AMA: Bruce!

BRUCE: Just take the taser Mum.

AMA: You're going to get hurt!

BRUCE: NO, YOU are gonna get hurt! Take it.

AMA: No!

BRUCE: Take the fucking taser Mum!

// BRUCE tries to force it into her hands, pushing AMA over.

TANYA: Bruce!

BRUCE: Sorry. It was an accident Mum. Man… I'm done here man, I'm gone!

AMA: Come back here! I'm talking to you.

Bruce!

Come back here!

Bruce!

TANYA: Mum, you okay?

// TANYA helps AMA up.

Just go I'll talk to him.

AMA: He's not listening! Tanya. Look at the time. I'm running late... Uhuru called a meeting this evening, a discussion on neighbourhood security. He says it's important. I'd ask Bruce to come but... You know what, I'm not going. Bruce come back down /

TANYA: Mum, go. I'll talk to him.

AMA: We have to sort this /

TANYA: Let him calm down first yeah?

AMA: I...you are right. Wait...so much of your father is in you. You are the cornerstone of this family... I wish you got to know him, you have his temperament. You are precious and blessed. God watches and nothing will happen to you. Don't be afraid. The police can handle this.

TANYA: Well, they still haven't caught him. Bruce has a point, we should have stopped him already. He's just... worried. I'll go talk to him.

// TANYA hugs AMA and goes after BRUCE.

Bruce? Bruce!

// AMA leaves the room, returns, stares, lifts the taser, tucks it in her bag and leaves. TANYA walks in after BRUCE.

TANYA: Mum's right. This thing is changing you. Maybe... you should stop?

BRUCE: It was an accident.

TANYA: I know but /

BRUCE: I need to know she can look after herself. Where's she gone?

TANYA: She said Uhuru called some meeting tonight?

BRUCE: Yeah...he asked me to come but they're just gonna sit and talk, not actually do anything. Right up Mum's street. Man she's stubborn.

TANYA: That's where you get it from.

BRUCE: Don't start.

TANYA: All I'm saying is she's started the class, she's trying.

BRUCE: Did you hear what she said? She's not taking it seriously Tan. Prays she never has to defend herself? What's the point? Wait. It's been four weeks since Mum joined right?

TANYA: Yeah.

BRUCE: Maybe we should test her then?

TANYA: What? How?

BRUCE: Your idea? Like you said, just scare her. All we've gonna do is jump out the bushes, see if she can handle it. After a whole month she should be decent, at least to push me back right? Just jump out and see?

TANYA: Naaa…it was a bad idea. I got choir tomorrow, three songs to learn…

BRUCE: Choir over Mum? You wanted to come out with me before right? This is it.

TANYA: Not sure…

BRUCE: Tanya, I just pushed Mum over. I did that. Never in a million years would I have… Maybe you're both right and it's changing me. I just gotta know she can handle herself. I need to. We can do it together…or you just keep a look out?

TANYA: If we do this Bruce, you stop, right? No more going out.

BRUCE: Okay…

TANYA: BRUCE?

BRUCE: Alright.

TANYA: Alright then. Okay.

BRUCE: Cool. Just wait for me yeah, I'll be back after class. We get changed and go?

TANYA: Yeah

BRUCE: Best idea ever Tan. Laters.

SMITHY: So, technically I was off duty. I'd clocked off, I was going home. Streets were empty, night had settled comfortably into the city. It was quiet, calm before storms and that inkling policeman intuition thing was tingling. Back in the day, we wore long cloaks but the practice was stopped, health and safety or something but I remember my mac lifted in the breeze and I felt comforted by the span of it, its weight on my shoulders. I drove round just checking for something, not knowing why or what I'd see. There'd been eight robberies, the neighbourhood was tense, I felt it whenever I walked the beat, a rising tensions, an expectation of violence, a fear and I'd had enough. Then I saw him running, pounding pavement, carrying a backpack, pelting down the streets and I thought not again, not on my watch, nothing is gonna happen to this kid. So, I stopped him.

Why you running?

BRUCE: That's my business?

SMITHY: I told you to stay off the streets.

BRUCE: Man, go catch a proper thief? Leave me alone.

SMITHY: What's in the bag Bruce?

BRUCE: Don't have time for this.

Move out my way.

Let me pass.

SMITHY: Against the wall.

BRUCE: Leave me alone!

SMITHY: Against the wall.

BRUCE: Don't touch my bag man, let me go.

SMITHY: Calm down. Stop struggling.

BRUCE: Let me go. Get off me. Get OFF ME.

SMITHY: I'll have to restrain you.

Calm down.

BRUCE: Mr Uhuru warned us about you lot. He's got plans for you. Big ones. Get off.

SMITHY: Calm down. Calm down.

BRUCE: We're coming for you. Get off man.

SMITHY: Shhhs

BRUCE: Can't breathe.

SMITHY: Shhhh…there…there. Calm down.

BRUCE: You're choking me.

SMITHY: A sleeper hold Commander. He'd wake with a slight headache, nothing else. It was for his own safety. I carried him into the squad car intending to take him home when he regained consciousness, drop him at his front door, keep him off the streets, but what he said stirred me "He's got plans for you. Big ones." We knew of this Uhuru Moses, bodyguard turned civilian leader. I drove to his gym just to check it out. Parked the squad car two streets down, slipped my baton into my pocket just incase, I mean he was a martial arts

47

master. Bruce was still unconscious. I went in and the gym was bustling, adults from the neighbourhood lined every wall, huddled in corners, sat facing the ring, on floor mats chatting, waiting for him and when he arrived it was like…nothing I'd ever seen. Silence took the room, spotlight in the ring and the things he talked about, all of them listening.

UHURU: The young ones who attend my class complain of stop and search powers, of police harassment; fear in their hearts. And those powers came when this government started their so called 'War on drugs'. They have been lying to us for centuries. When you can, on your computers, your mobile devices, research the Anglo-Chinese Wars, known as the Opium Wars. By 1839, the British Government had set up factories in India to create an addictive drug. Our government were selling an estimated 40,000 chests of Opium along the coast of China. Unregulated, direct drug trafficking. The Chinese emperor, fed up of seeing the destruction to his country, his community, banned the selling of Opium. What did our government do? The British Government started a war. Such was their military might that the Emperor surrendered. They invaded, massacred and killed so they could sell drugs, unchallenged, to the Chinese people. Imagine. Bare faced hypocrisy.

The police humiliate us on our own streets, intimidate our own youth, put fear in our own hearts. In the Middles East, where as you know I've lived, a nation this government is allied with, Israel, send troops to harass and ransack the homes of innocent Palestinians, to make examples of them, parade them through streets, line them up, humiliate them, put fear in the hearts of other Palestinians watching behind drawn curtains so they are too afraid to rise up. Why do I mention Palestine? Because all things are linked, because our police do the same thing. Fear is the worst of human emotions, it immobilises us. That's why we aren't out hunting the mugger who has terrorised our community. Eight victims, three hospitalised. Instead we are indoors. Afraid of the mugger, of police who are meant to defend us. Their task is to uphold the hypocritical laws of this land; to enforce government's will on the people. They don't care about us.

AMA: These are your opinions. You have no proof; the police are just people.

UHURU: Everything I've said is documented, online. I'm just joining dots. As for police, they say crowds don't blush. It's institutional. Mob mentality. We go missing in their custody, some of us never breathe again /

AMA: They're not all like that.

UHURU: Not one should be like that! We shouldn't 'hope' we meet a good one! It's unacceptable /

AMA: There are bad apples in all barrels /

UHURU: If we don't act we will all turn rotten, suspicious of ourselves, our neighbourhoods…listen, I've trained you the best I can, with enough skills to disarm most, if not all assailants. You are effective as the average officer and as locals, better qualified to police our streets, our neighbourhoods. I say we don't need their hypocrisy, don't need their intimidation, don't need them infecting the seeds of our community. Every time you come training, you achieve step one of what I am about to propose. It's simple. It's what they claim to do for us, which now we must do ourselves. We have to present a united front, so Step 1: Wear a uniform. Step 2: Protect what you love, who you care about. 3: Let nothing get in your way. Over the coming weeks I will distribute leaflets; aims, objectives, targets, goals, ways to go about achieving this. We may face opposition but make no mistake, together we are unstoppable. Thanks for coming. See you soon.

TANYA: I waited for you at home but you never came. Bruce, you weren't there. You couldn't do it, so I did it. We've always been a team. All I've gotta do, you said that night, all you're gonna do is jump out the bushes, see if Mum can handle it. After a whole month she should at least push back right? It was simple. I put on dark clothes, scarf over my face, dressed to blend in with the night and went after Mum, went to the class and watched them talking through the window. I almost fell asleep it was so boring. Kept pinching my legs so they wouldn't go numb.

SMITHY: I couldn't believe what I was hearing Commander. I stood outside, trembling as they filed out, chatting excitedly, thinking how much I sacrificed for this job, these people I walked past, day in day out. They just see the uniform, never the man. I was dazed, I walked to the bus stop. Didn't know where to begin, how to combat his arguments…what to think of myself.

TANYA: Finally, it was over and they came out in groups. I follow them, thinking what would Bruce do, tried to walk like you, make my feet fall like dust on the pavement, pressing into shadows, must have looked stoopid! They got to the bus stop.

SMITHY: Yes I was confused, but did that cloud my judgement? Never Commander, even when they arrived and I engaged them in discussion, I talked with a clear mind.

// All are heated.

AMA: I heard what you said Uhuru, but your arguments are flawed. The police protect us.

UHURU: We've gone over this before.

AMA: Run it by me again?

TANYA: Headlights kept catching me out and I thought Mum had seen me a couple times trailing after her but she was too busy chatting with Mr Moses.

UHURU: They exist to administer the will of the state. They are designed to safeguard the state. The state, not the people.

AMA: The state is the people.

UHURU: No, the state is what holds the people. It is the cage. It is the pressure cooker, the container. We are the ones who do not fit. We do not cage easily. If the state works against us, we must work against the state.

// SMITHY laughs.

TANYA: I waited, only half breathing, only half seeing, only half hearing, but making Mum out in the flickering florescent bus stop light, the bin spilling parking tickets, leaflets and tissues across the street.

AMA: Do you know what you're proposing? Have you thought it through? How will we fund such a thing?

UHURU: Sacrifices, small contributions. Each member of the community gives a percentage of his or her monthly wage.

AMA: So basically, tax? We pay enough of that.

UHURU: But this will directly benefit /

AMA: Uhuru, I've listened to you, but I think it is unfeasible.

SMITHY: Listen to the woman.

TANYA: I was hiding, trying to stop the bushes rustling in the moon light.

UHURU: Pardon?

SMITHY: Nothing.

AMA: And what about the officers who will lose their jobs?

SMITHY: Yeah what about them?

UHURU: Who are you?

SMITHY: A concerned citizen.

UHURU: This is a private conversation, it doesn't concern you.

SMITHY: You're having it in a public space and /

TANYA: They started quarrelling, some guy yelling at Mr Moses, shaking his fists and Mum telling them to shush.

AMA: Have we met before?

SMITHY: No. I don't think so. Now, Mr Moses, your proposal is preposterous. We will not accept any such /

AMA: You were at the event today weren't you?

UHURU: Who do you mean by 'We'?

SMITHY: We who police this land, these streets, take our jobs very seriously.

UHURU: Ama, stand back from this lunatic.

SMITHY: We execute the law with utmost clarity.

UHURU: How many black men have died in police custody? Is that your clarity?

SMITHY: We cannot be held responsible for the actions of a few

UHURU: Stop and Search policy? You treat entire communities as criminals because of the actions of a few.

AMA: Gentlemen, calm down.

SMITHY: That is a preventative measure.

AMA: Uhuru, step back from the policeman.

UHURU: You want to prevent crime? First, stop supporting a system that directly necessitates crime; politicians who are criminals, companies breaking tax laws /

SMITHY: That is a separate issue.

UHURU: Really? Let me link them for you.

// TANYA walks into their conversation.

TANYA: And… Action!

TANYA: I jumped out at Mum and she got proper shook, fell on the ground and I had to concentrate so I wouldn't laugh, had to make it look real and the knife I was holding was shining in the light. Mum kept looking at it and I thought she'd recognise it from the kitchen so I griped it tighter, flashed it in her face. She was looking at me and I didn't notice when the men stopped talking. Mum was reaching into her bag and I lowered the knife just a little, just a touch, to say Mum don't give me your purse! Don't give in that quickly, gotta fight! What's Mr Moses teaching you? And Mr Moses' leg flashed past my head and the second one was coming fast. The other guy pulled out a baton from nowhere and he was coming at me, swinging it above his head and I got scared and ran to Mum but she had a black thing in her hand, the taser we made, the blue line of electricity fizzling and she was coming as well and…it worked. Mum defended herself. They all did.

// SMITHY pulls back the scarf revealing a wounded TANYA. BRUCE runs on stage.

BRUCE: Tan…

I'm so sorry… Shoulda been there.

TANYA: You couldn't.

BRUCE: Shoulda been me.

TANYA: Then you'd be lying here bleeding into your body.

BRUCE: Better me than you.

TANYA: No Bruce. You were just trying to /

BRUCE: It was my fault. Wasn't it?

TANYA: No.

BRUCE: The doctors can't stop it Tanya, the bleeding…
they can't make you better.

This is all on me.

TANYA: It's not your fault.

BRUCE: Not Mum… I can't go after her.

TANYA: It was all of them. You can't get everyone.

BRUCE: Someone's gotta pay!

TANYA: I have… I've paid.

BRUCE: So sorry Tan.

TANYA: You've just gotta talk to Mum. She's gonna need
you. More than ever.

*// AMA enters the room. BRUCE wipes his face, they stare
at each other, AMA is in tears. BRUCE makes for the door.*

TANYA: Where are you going?

BRUCE: Get some water. Would you like some… Mum?

AMA: Yes. Thank you.

*// BRUCE pauses to take off his hoodie. Folds and gives it to
TANYA. AMA walks to her.*

END.

WWW.OBERONBOOKS.COM

Follow us on www.twitter.com/@oberonbooks
& www.facebook.com/OberonBooksLondon